A *Journey* within

A *Journey* within

TARUN

PARTRIDGE
A Penguin Random House Company

To order additional copies of this book, contact
Partridge India
000 800 10062 62
orders.india@partridgepublishing.com

www.partridgepublishing.com/india

Contents

This book is to:

My Children:
Pallavi: In deepening my insight,
Sangeeta and Pankaj:
For strengthening my wisdom.
Upali and Himanshu for expanding
my heart and finally my
Wife, Meeta to understanding intricacies of life.

MY HEARTFELT THANKS

In the Publication of my Poems, I owe my heartfelt thanks to my following friends with whom I have been sharing my Poems for quite sometime. Never ever had planned its publication but for Shree Rajendra Babu (Shree Rajendra Kishore Panda, is an eminent Poet, Scholar and Novelist of Odissa), probably no serious thought to its publication would have entered my mind. I have been as distant as close to him and his advice gave me the courage to get over my reservation for its publication and I owe this publication to him.

Shree Vinod Kumar Shukla apart from being an eminent Poet and Novelist, has always commanded respect and admiration for his contribution to enriching literature. Yet, its not only his creative eminence in creativity has earned it but in being a person he is. His simplicity is overwhelmingly magnetic that drew me to him and more I learnt of him, my respect and affection only grew. His appreciation of my Poems only reinforced Rajendra Babu's advice.

Dr. J. P. Das in hearing of my wish to publishing of my Poems happily added further strength to my wish. Dr Das, an eminent Poet and Novelist, his contribution to Odiya Literature been pretty rich as much as his passion for creativity that has never set to any boundary. His simplicity also has a magnetic pull and his encouragement for the publication cleared the path to decision.

Shree Satyananda Mishra despite being a bureaucrat of great repute always had time to living his passion for sharing creativity.

A voracious reader, his interests been never confined to any boundary though his passion for Art and literature been overwhelmingly on the plus side. Its he, who Led me to understanding of what is not as against what is, which in turn shaped my understanding of creativity and channelizing my passion. It has always been a joy to share his observation in the appreciation of art and literature. I owe this Publication to him as much as to others.

Dr Sushil Trivedi's passion for Art and Literature is inherited from his father who was an eminent Poet. I have known Dr Trivedi closely for more than five decades and hence had the opportunity to know his father from whom I learnt what simplicity is. Dr Sushil Trivedi has been a balancing factor in shaping of my approach to creativity and of its continuance. He has truly been as much a support for this publication.

I joyfully offer to sharing my Poems to lovers of Poetry.

Tarun Kanungo

1

WHERE DO I GO FROM HERE

Where do I go from here?
Know not where.
Neither know where to
My next step may carry me.
Who it be that
Ignites craving ceaseless?
Never knowing why and
Neither to where?
Who it is that provokes and
Who is it that responds?
And where from
It gathers momentum that
So cruelly bursts forth within?

II

It ought to be in me.
I am sure.
At some place it must be, but where?
Know it not and know not why.
It surfaces chameleon-like frequent;
Changing color at will that
rise fast to varying scale.
Varying equally in intensity,
Design and color that
Penetrate deep into veins.
Suck up blood leech-like and
Leave it to bleed its end...
Know not, if I can ever
Comprehend its moves that
Emerge as fast as it vanishes.
Cutting me through ugly grooves
frequent all over and
Dump me helpless, clueless,
Dumb and dazed at nowhere.
Playing at will with life as if
It be a plaything to play as
Whims and fancy dictate.
Guess it must be a devil in me
Playing its game before
devouring its prey.

III

Yet, whatever it be,
I relish not that erupt to
Stir me wild; Burst forth
Into a whirlwind wherein
Caught in its vortex,
Wildly spun get thrown
Onto a dreadful strange land.
Get tangled in its net where
Intrigue reigns mighty.
However hard I may rake my head,
It just turn into waste to seeking escape.
Dumbfounded lost,
Bewildered and dazed,
Know not if I ever can escape
It's intriguing riddle to freedom!

IV

Questions chasing through birth have
Grown diabolical in time though
It carries sum and substance none.
They have grown big in size and stature.
Devoid of vision act petty like
dog chasing its tail.
Oh, I am dog-tired, chasing shadows constant
In hail and rain, over mountains and deserts.
Unceasingly haunted by the restless ghost within that
Cursed and deluded, smothered and lost,
Breathing in stale breath, palm rubbing hard to
Survive almost paralyzing freezing cold.
Wonder if ever playing this game
I would ever glow back to regaining life's spark?

V

Irrespective of what it may or may not be,
Obsession digging deep in vein
Erupts sudden to carrying both- world and beyond.
Thrown on to the world to playing its game to
Amass it all to grow in name and fame.
Matters little whether it be sane or insane!
Ways of the World centered in gain looks down at
Anything less that be not worthy to aim.
Worldly spirit all the same must grow and expand.
Stand out mighty in focus defined best despite
All intrigue confound and perpetuate to
Denying it all, defying fate. Life thrown to
Wild waves must swim over to other side.
In being a success adorned with victory to
Own the world as well the invisible other.
After all it's the pride earned that matters to
Let its feathers gracefully wave to the world
Glowing proud on cap to adorning the head.

VI

But then how do I lead life to its source to end
All cravings that stick all over restlessness bred?
It stretches endless. Propel me wild grown mad?
Path that appear cool tempting and straight vanish
Sudden to reappear into U-pin bend.
Yet, it leads next to hit a dead end. Blank and void.
Sitting dumb gazing quiet far into the sky wish
I were a bird with mighty wings to
Measure the immeasurable at ease flying
Endless to being its beginning.
Pointed sharp tireless to shooting like a dart to
Rid all mystery that intrigues the heart to grow
Beyond that strike love and hate to
Reap out duality tearing it apart.
Ending all life was wasted in lured to chase,
Ending that life was wasted to drift apart to
Happily merge in the Whole in being its part.

2

TREE AND THE BIRD

The Tree And the Bird
Once upon a time,
there was a small lone tree
on the bank of a small river.
Being an insignificant one,
it attracted none.
A small bird lived on it.
Tree loved it.
Every morning lovingly watched it
fly across the sky.
and was back on to the tree
in the evening to rest.
Tree longed to talk to the bird,
to talk sweet things
to make the bird feel at home.
Sometime bird sang that delighted the tree.
It almost made it cry in joy.
Bird never knew tree had a heart.

-2-

Every morning even before sunrise
bird flew off
as all birds do.
Tree looked at it with joy,
and waited anxiously
for the evening to arrive
and when it did, tree felt so happy.
sometime the bird returned late.
it made tree grow apprehensive.
It kept gazing at the sky, revolving its eyes
all around,
and-when spotted the bird-at a distant sky
shooting straight towards it,
tree flew into ecstasy.
It fluttered its branches joyfully
to welcome the bird.
The bird never knew tree had a heart.

-3-

One evening-while tree waited
the bird returned along with
an another bird,
together they made a nest.
And the bird
laid some eggs,
sat over it
for longer period.
After some time
young little ones
popped out of eggs.
Tree loved to have them, and-
looked after them,
when mother and father bird
flew away to get food
for the young ones.
Tree joyfully watched
the young ones grow.
Loved to listen to their twittering.
flapping off little wings sensing
their parent's return.

As they grew
little older
wings grown stronger,
were taught to fly.
Soon they could fly
on their own.
One day,
they flew out
and did not return.
The couple as usual
did return to the tree,
sad and aloof,
missing the young ones.
Sat quiet through the night,
with no song to sing.
Tree didn't know
What to say
to comfort
the grieving birds.
It silently cried
for the birds,
in not being able
to share their grief.
The birds
never saw
welled up eyes of the tree,
to feel its heart.

- 4 -

One morning,
as usual,
both the birds flew away,
and as usual,
tree anxiously
waited for their return.
As the evening approached,
it kept rolling its eyes
back and forth,
revolving
in all direction,
looking for the couple
in the sky
only to see nothing.
It grew sad.

Yet, quite late,
it heard a flutter of wings,
stretching its eyes
in the dark,
it felt the bird's return,
but all alone.
And as it sat
where it always did
it felt sad,
and the tree
could hear it crying.
Once again the tree
knew not what to say,
and it bled as much
as the bird.
Bird never knew of it.

- 5 -

On the touch of
The next morning,
bird flew away
as usual.
Tree waited.
Evening arrived
Yet it found.
no sign of the bird.
Tree kept rolling
its eyes in the sky, and-
soon it grew dark
Bird did not return.
Morning came
And day passed,
evening came and night fell,
bird did not return.

Day in and out,
heart in its mouth,
longingly tree
stayed in wait,
hoping against all odds
for bird's return.
But it did not.
Tree grew sadder.
It felt,
river bank has
suddenly grown
ever
so lonely.

- 6 -

Summer came,
hotter than ever.
River dried up,
so did the world around.
Tree knew not
what choked within,
to cry aloud.
Looking at heaven felt,
it never knew
what it lived for so long
and why?
It sensed it has stood
millions of years
on the river bank,
and felt it had
outlived all wish to live.
It knew for sure,
day would
Continue to burn, and-
bird would never return.

-7-

One day-
early in the morning
axe of a woodcutter
fell mighty on its trunk.
It bled
Within and out,
Yet, refused
to acknowledge
emerging pain.
Sighed not
as it fell lifeless
on the river bed.
Scorching rays of the sun
had dried up
not only the river bed,
but sign of life
all around.
There was no tree
On the river bank that
lived to love.

3

NEVER TO REACH NO WHERE

Half is not full though
Full can be divided into
Half and half, or
Into quarters or
into one third or
as you may wish.

Full divided is never full,
And the world is divided
One end to another
Not in 1/2 or
1/4 or 1/3
But in as many.
Almost countless.
should it interest,
you may count untired
holding patience intact for
it shall tire you all the same.

Take a little rest and start all over.
You would still be counting
Until count is lost.
In counting out fatigue won't
Let you to keep eyes open.

This is the World we live in.
This is the World
We translate living
In high lofty words.
In billions and trillions.
As may whims and fancy dictate that
Sets one against the other,
Cook reasons to be just
Justifying all unjustifiable as
Mode set define wisdom of violence.
Or we may as recluse
live to comprehend
The Incomprehensible.
Singing out in tune forced that can't be sung...

Its been what it is.
On and on and on.
Life after life.
An unending race.
Never to reach nowhere.

4

HEADING RIGHT

I think I am heading right.
I am smiled at on the road by
Friends and strangers alike.
My heart tells me I am on right road
In being able to smile back clean in
Naturally feeling warm to respond that
I see all around and
I feel mighty happy to see
world has grown sane in me,
Animate, inanimate all.

I stop by in seeing children playing.
It always makes me happy stealing
Joy in their play. In all they do.
The little child throws the ball at me
And giggles in hitting me right.
I laugh back.

The world in me gets infected by
the mischief innocence plays.
Mother's concern motherly smiles.
I pick up the kid in my arms.
My joy multiplies in being objected not.
The child giggles in being picked up and
Child's mischief giggles in me.
Only children have the knack of
Striking it right and it tells
I am heading right.
In being washed clean.
I can't go wrong when
love holds me in arms at every step.
I am happy heading right
Carrying life and the World
Happily together in me.

5

GAZING AT LIFE

Wandering eyes of loneliness
Staring out of window,
Often gets centered
At the jet black, bared naked tree.
Weather beaten rough that
Bared to the skin appear
Dried up almost dead.
It stands tall all alone within itself,
Paradoxically midst
Spread out abundant greenery
Luxuriously spread all over.
Far and near.
In and around.

Gaze shift inward on to the mirror
Wherein I see me to being the tree.
Gripped in loneliness standing alone
Midst wilderness wearing a lost vacant look;
Focused at nothing,
Chasing nothingness that
Never got to nowhere ever to
Achieve spark up life.

A sudden jolt returns to
Looking out of window that
Blows me to shame in seeing tree afresh;
Fighting alone to vagaries of life.
Beaten black and blue over and over
In being Inflicted rough constant
Through and through yet,
It broods not. Stands tall in being itself.
And I, racing to become lost to being I am!
Shame soaked I dare not look at the mirror.
In that it multiplies fast like crows
flock on to dead that
Beak hard, chewing and cawing constant,
Hit merciless hard onto flesh.
My hands reach for the head
Pulling hair insanity grabbed.....

Looking back, remember not when I last laughed,
Neither when mirror glowed to my smile,
And one that I wear proud despises itself.
Crawling in shoes that never fitted well.
Yet, repeatedly I polished it to shine it best
To hold me tall to being I am not.

Gazing at the tree; It stares back
Screening me thorough and through.
Penetrated deep into my pores it
Pours out scorn over and over
Onto that wears shoes to reflecting face.....
Strange, against I would wish:
I Fall in love with the tree drawing strength
From its oneness in that it stands tall.
Seeking nothing from heaven nor prays.

Looking at the tree only after few days,
I am struck hard amazed
In that my roving eyes detect;
Tree wearing sudden a new look
Graced with few tender leaves.
More reddish than green,
Adoring its only branch drooping low
With a spark of sudden burst of life that
Only few days back I swear
Was all bare and naked dried up dead.

Seeing in the seen thrown off guard.....
I would hardly have believed
Had not my eyes witnessed it.
Faith persisted over destiny
Changed its course to
Rekindle it to shine forth to life.
Tender leaves fluttered cool adorned by
Breeze blowing soft and sweet.

I look at my face in the mirror and
See it all in being caught in the web...
Know not who I am that to standing tall
Fall on to shoes painfully polished to
Shine mirror like to heighten stature.

6

IN EXPLORING THE ROOT OF NAME

i.

I often wonder at the root of name.
Its origin to it being invented wherein
Life is more or less, summed up to being.
That the holder holds dear holding in it all.
A picture of life projected to being,
Be it or not, in that it visibly reflects its colors,
Whatever it be, fair or dark,
Black, yellow, brown...
Its class and creed to that it belongs.
Even to explore further;
Calculating out details in
Adding, deducting, multiplying,
As well that may be needed to
Calculate further to route through,
Be it algebraic or geometrical to

Carve out the pertinent in the name.
Jolly well to let all emerge, facts and fiction
From A to Z.

ii.

Often I feel, what it would have been like,
Had my name was different than
I am held in, or had no name at all?
How the constellation up above
had acted and reacted to casting their spell?
Be it for better or worse, would it have
Placed me different, to think and feel,
Act and react to facing different all that
Puzzle and dazzle thrown in?
Be it reward or blow, joy or sufferings or
Questions that be difficult to face,
Would it have been all different than
as of now I do?
I know, I am as much in the name in being
As breath be to hold me alive.
Yet, I know not what it would have been like
Had it not be the name I cling to that
Propel, stall, push and pull, shrink or stretch to
Know myself in it that I succeed and fail and
Fall easy often to see it all

Through the eyes of others to
knowing who I am, in that name projects me to
Share the pride or shame or whatever it be that
The history in relation act on to reveal that
I can never sever may what I do as
It clings to my being like a lump that
Uncomfortably sticks out over my being.
Be it reward or blow that
Inflate or deflate,
Wherein my lineage get projected as far
It can expand and stretch the identity in
The name holds wherein
Head is either held high or hangs in shame.

iii.

Yet, the void strangely centered within
Stir and persist constant.
As much to confuse who may I be that
Reflected to being in the name that
Bounce back and forth as time adds on adding
In layer over layers,
In that it is reflected varying its contours
That prompt fresh survey of land it stands on to
add or deduct to being midst that fluctuate.
It's in the many that I get lost in being

Thrown into vortex of insoluble that
remain unresolved endless.
Name held in its grip projected
Far in excess to it actually be.

iv.

Wonder what it would have been
if Lotus wasn't known as Lotus or
rose hadn't grown to fame by its name?
Would named different had made any
Tangible difference to be other than they do?
Impacting its look and aroma in its fragrance?
For that reason, say, tigers weren't called tiger ;
would it have made them different than they are?
In being nameless had the man been different?
Be it more or less to being human
or still into lesser beings?
I know the question is cheeky but
Living it in name, it's the name grows tall
In that connected to that name governs?
In being with the World to live and act

Through its impulses that carry and
push me to live its passion
That may seemingly look sane
but invariably act insane.
Sharpening out cunning in
Matching tunes to its chosen rhythms
That time projects and demands.
In order to tide over every onslaught
time and again it is flung with
That don't match the name in that the holder resides.

v.

I am that in being I am.
Though in that I may or may not be.
Yet, arrogance strive to induce the wind to
Follow its sail to where ever it heads
irrespective of weather be.
Hence, I wonder, despite being human,
the drift that has taken me far
from that I was born into,
I am sure, it wasn't to grow into what I have;
Ruthless in honing skill, sharpening wits to
Let its identity grow strong in me to
Match the name to meeting its demand.

vi.

In the lure of freedom now it dawns that
It was a mere picture cleverly conceived.
That camouflage ugliness. I understand it now.
Truth being Truth never can be bent.
No matter how clever be the artist to
Put forth its mighty talents to claim,
truth at the end always bursts forth
Tearing out the canvas its painted on.
Truth is, unalterable dynamic
In that it ever remains unbendable intact.
Be it storm, tornado or tsunami to sweep it all clean,
Living in name is living in pretension that
Severs it with that truth hold that drag it away
Further and further from the whole.
Wonder how the identity aspirations
Works amongst life in the wild
That vary as wildly in shape and size and style,
Be it a crow or sparrow, tiger or a boar,
Hawks or owl or be it elephants or rhino
That live nameless in the wild.
Wonder, if they were tied to a name like man,
would the wild live different in them?
Would it simplify their life?
Would it be any more than it has helped man?

Who in getting to know all knows not himself.
Will it be better than their own uncanny way to
Live in to being themselves to being whole.
Seeking must be the most unholy that
severs the whole into part.
Boosting fallen out expanded into the false.
To exhibit and project that is not.
Life naturally differs to living in the wild in being
Unpretentious in being itself, living
full to its inherent passion,
Undivided within and out, free of
any drawn out boundary.
Integrated within, its identity rests in being itself.

vii.

In being the name identity is secured
But the nameless tide sore high
That aspire not severance from the source.
It can't, for it belongs to that;
That eternally ecstasy drenched
Division itself is the part of the Whole.

7

HOME COMING OF MY SON

I eagerly wait on Thursday for
My son's return home
Having eagerly waited through the week but
Time in total disregard to my eagerness
Stretches it longer moving
Even slower than a snail.
I wish it moved faster.
But I understand the game wish play.
I try not to mind.
Wait being well worth the pain.

Thursday must be a good day to
Keep my eyes glued to sky. I only
Hope weather turns not bad for
My son to land at home safe, yet,
Apprehension keeps me on guard.
Who can tell of what may happen.
Hence I keep all reactions at hold,
Keeping my fingers crossed I keep
All reactions at hold except eyes that
Restlessly keep staring at the sky.

I couldn't live pretending to change things.
I know change take place unwarned on its own.
Beyond and beside me, waits for none.
Hence I wish not to invest my energy in hope.
So much so feel I must get through it and beyond.
I keep pinching my skin often to stay aware lest
hope creeps in unnoticed when not on guard.
I have to start with doing away to counting that
Centers me to calculating, plus and minuses that
Engross ceaseless into division and multiplication;
draw me to figure out profit and
loss in the transacted.
Oh, I feel so good to figure a way to rid of it...
And to ensure, shout often in my ear to tell
I carry no heart in business no more, yet
Proposition surface often to lure.....
I look at it not in being desperate to
get past of it all to living free to
Relish freedom more than the word.
It appeared up front in the beginning
A tall order to cope.
Old grooves weren't making it easy and
Effort did never no good except compounding it.
Hence I opted to stay away from it cool.
Just walked through without ever
Looking back at the crowd that gather
In protest mind collected to doing well in life.

I only hope whatever happens to be good since
Bad mounting heavy been overflowing through ages.
I know option to be none and hence
Look up at heaven to bless me the strength to
Bear the fall of hammers as and when it does
Without any tremor..

Yet, habit draws me to keep looking at sky
Even though I resist hard.
Old grooves have its way to attack,
It's because weather change makes me apprehensive.
I am although aware reacting is meaningless for
It stretches on and on to a dead end.
Let weather turn as it may please.
My son would for sure
Find his way home safe.

Up above somewhere, I feel in my guts
Connected with the nameless that
Reverberate thriving all over
In thousands of names.
Who knows and does it all right.
a l w a y s.
Befittingly to be best for all
Including my son's home coming.

8

A DIALOGUE

Tell me my friend,
How do you live your multiple images
One in another as well simultaneous in many?
Chameleon like yet without changing color that
you enter at ease as may your sensor hint.
Changing gears faster than odds can cope,
Irrespective of terrain you are on.
Knowingly well, within you,
You are not you that your images project but
Rooted different altogether than that
Transplant anew into growing hybrid in you.
Though born and brought up normal
As most children but grew taller in frame to
Break away easy stepping into shoes that
Neither fitted you nor belonged, yet,
Devil inspired dared you to
Reach your envied top and
I see you have.

Tell me what be the next my friend?
I see shoes stepped into has worn out,
Wearing you out as well.
It reflects clear on your face.
Those little wrinkles that were
Almost invisible appear visibly bold.
It can't measure up to your future moves but
Knowing you, I am sure,
You must be in look out for shoes that
You can step in as easy as been so far.

You have sold your wares easy and well so far.
I notice it in all your outbursts. I also see,
Your eyes look so distant;
Perhaps to measuring up horizon to go beyond.
You reflect harmony almost personified in
Rolling out your acts sailing smooth,
Despite it amply reflects ugliness on your person.
That onlookers eyes don't see in the act that
Reflect merely a fraction of the invisible whole
Cleverly hidden as skin over flesh
and flesh over bones.
Which clothed further tastefully to matching trend or
Your chosen style to match your acts.
Added to it you have your bewitching smile to
Carve out the day with ample
safeguard to your image.
Eyes see what it sees but can't travel beyond and
You my friend understand it so very well to

A JOURNEY WITHIN

Setting out the day in your chosen mold to
Selling lure to expanding your market.
Underneath you perpetuate nurturing that's ugly.
Carefully keeping the watchful eyes at bay.
As an extra measure to further safeguard it all,
You hit hard to disarming odds with such skill that
None can fathom you beyond your skin.

You know it my friend and I indeed admire you...
How cleverly you hide the ugly safely tucked in
Your masterly built cocoon impregnable almost that
Let you scheming in comfort to
Dreaming of all that lie ahead to
Sailing smooth carried by soft breeze
Lazily on dancing waves...

Tell me my friend:
With all feathers in your cap,
How do you feel in being where you are?
Do you ever wake up to taking a look at that
Left behind all through yester years?
Does it reel out your beginning until date?
Does it carry you back to the days you learnt to trot?
And how temptation led you
stepped into various shoes
That never fitted nor belonged to you?
Does silence ever hit you deep to return to it?
Stirred of emotion does it ever
cause you any pinprick?
Of all love and care and concern poured over you

Snapped at ease as if it meant nothing to you?
Do you ever feel in being that you are not?
Do you ever ponder over the cost to
Reaching where you are?

I guess not.
You have gone too far ahead.
Far above all ties in
Holding on to that, that
Holds you in its steely grip.
You can't loosen it even if you wish.
Any emotional jolts, I know,
No big deal for you to handle.
You jerk it away like a speck of dust on you.
Bravo, your rise been far faster than I guessed.
How easily you reflect indifference to it all.
Yet, my friend, however clever you may act to
Cheating yourself, tell me barring that visible,
What actually you have gained?
I can see deep within you, you are shaken
In the heart of your heartless heart.
Though you have mastered your smile that
Hid you safe in the act you stage.
Mere your twitch of lips cow down the risen waves.
Knowing looks deceptive;
You understand your friends and foes so well that
Even your stretched up smile
Strike bolt out of blue to hit up a storm to
Blow away those who stand against.

Sure, I see, its not for nothing
You have honed your skill flawless to
Polish the granite within you to perpetually shine.
You know cast out layer of the snake is not the snake.
Hence to play doubly safe you
Never cast out any layer, Do you my friend?
On the contrary, you go on adding over the old
To stay miles away from harms way.
You must be proud of your talents my friend with
All the tools you keep always up your sleeve to
Act flawless like an expert surgeon which you are
With your penetrating eagle's eyes
Clubbed with a lion's heart and yet
Have smooth ladies' smooth finger to
Handle the most delicate surgery.
You have it all in you my friend and to
Top it further have a jackal's head and
Hyena's jaw and as paradox would have it;
You have honey dripping lips that
Makes the surgery smooth and painless
Under your concocted anesthetic spell.

No my friend, I am not being
crooked and neither out to
Dissect you threadbare intend to skinning you to
Make you to stand more than naked.
Though in being frank, I would wish to.
I breathe along your breath my friend.
Be it day or night, awake or asleep and

I am not your shadow.
Neither been close nor been away.
I am you, in you and yet I am not
You ever cared to own?
Its too late anyway and
Any question of kind is irrelevant, hence
You keep me shut under the cocoon
Specially built for me lest I rise up to jeopardize
Your mission tainting your image to
Placing you naked on the cross.
Attracting crowd to see you
Through and through inside out.
I know you would prefer to take me for dead.
You have wringed my head umpteen times, but
Know my friend, I live still and
Would live till your last to
See it all through to the end.
You are not likely to end soon for I see,
You still have some length of spring to breathe.
But let it be known to you my friend;
It would not always be spring to last you forever.
With the onset of autumn,
Trees shall shed their leaves to wearing anew.
When would you shed yours my
friend to wearing new?
Seasons are meant to change and
You may not be very far from your autumn,
And soon it would be winter,
I know you would wish to stretch it longer

To perpetuate in your sadistic glow to
Make me bear the brunt of your repeated blast that
You blow ruthless over and over to
Multiply my wound that never heal.
It would not I know, until
You finally end up to breathe your last.
When your cocoon would bursts forth
In its own ugliness triggered by its own stink
And then it shall reel you out your journey
From cradle to burning pyre.
I assure, I would step aside when it does.
Standing close yet far to witnessing it all.
It would make me sad yet happy for
I see the promise of dawn in the Sun set to
Breathe afresh fresh air
Blowing through life soft and cool.

9

IN BEING TIED TO THE POST

Growing up been packed with
Earned unearned never sought after learning that
Perhaps teachers the preachers and do-gooders and
All likeminded collective duty bound
Poured down my throat claiming
Living it would set life to living right.
The foremost being, above all to
Make God happy.

Conditioned to living order of the taught,
Moving carefully in measured steps,
Reflecting it's spirit in all my gestures,
Never knowing why and where to it led.
Setting aside all offshoot,
I grew rooted strong to living right.
Never knowing what it meant that
Inter-played into living right, though

Often heart missed beats to
Feeling at home that
Neither had the Sun nor Moon ever to
Glowing over roof nor ever could sitting cool
Under the blue sky floated along
The soft breeze singing out heart.

And I grew up never grown.
Shackled and tied to wilderness that
Spread over abundant in and around,
Stitched apprehension into nerves constant.
And I cried helpless crying loud that grew
Louder still in being torn apart.
Leave me alone, I heard me burst;
I break all shackles herein and now.
I would let my son grow free, act free to
Breathing free to grow mighty wings to
Flying free at will as sky unfolds path
Fearless into unknown as wings
Set wide open unconditionally free.

10

TO FIND MY HAVEN AS GOD MAY HAVE PLANNED

In that all grew that led to
Matching the ways of the world,
I grew fast tired in me to
matching all its equations that made me
Running to chase this and that.
It has thoroughly drained me out flat.
Let it be known to all who teach that
I herewith refuse to digest it any more.

Lying in the open under
Vast spread of mighty sky
In pondering over it all,
The blue evening suddenly
Lit up in me sudden freeing me of it all and
I was lost under the glitter of
Countless bewitching stars that
Delightfully absorbed me in them to
Gazing at the abstraction wherein

The part built in me expanded into the whole.
Transported to a zone far away from known that
Led me into trance lost in heavenly glory.
Fully absorbed, freed of mind's scrutiny.
So much so that it seemed no concern to me to
Being dead or alive.
Hardly had any clue of time and space as
Stars above gently pulled me further
Up into their midst to roam free
Joyfully drifting unbound by will.
Happiness sizzled as heart burst in joy.
Never ever had tasted such sweetness before.
I was up riding horses formed in flaming clouds that
Galloped soundless through starlit sky and
I felt to being a celestial being far, far away from
Home and the Worldly shackles.
All apprehension melted free as it
Shattered all threatening bolts out of blue.
Before I could figure out, I was ecstatically lifted
Up and up and still up above on to a different plane,
Beyond mind's reach where senses just floated
Wrapped up in ecstasy, nay, in being it.

What is it that made me to deserve it all, I wondered,
Desperate I looked for the cause in the effect that
Rid me off of all earthly chain, wherein
My own little self was its exalted own to
Breathe loud and free just as I would wish to
Play as I wished befriended by all.
Playing with elephants, tigers,
Deer and wolves and birds and all as
One plays with its dog.
Running and chasing butterflies,
Flying at will high up in sky,
Up onto tall trees midst chirping birds
Looking fondly at all to ridding all dread to
Let joy ooze free in all hearts in
Pronounced togetherness in being never alone.
Singing heart loud, sailing on winds
Breaking all barriers setting all free to
Being in all as well all held in me.
Far away from dread of routine network built that
Siege me still while breathing free.

It strikes shiver by its thought alone...
I have fervently prayed addressing all angels
Not knowing how must I pray to God yet I did
All in His name anyway to bless me out of dread.
A way out to be in midst of all,
Wherein I grow and glow to being myself
Without being pushed to becoming x y z,
Dragged into the lure that great men poured,
That teachers inspired on the strength of burrowed
Roared to cast me into this and that, that
Led me to losing I am.

Oh, I am tired of being taught constant
To doing this and that to becoming great,
How can life be a mere guided tour that
Agitate heart pushing mind to revolt,
No, I wish not pushed to be programmed,
Spelt out to imitate to becoming great to
Trading my soul to glamorize cage.
In being that I know I am not and neither
Acting it out ever been my cup of tea.
Hence mighty teachers of the world I pray:
Leave me alone to wander my world midst star to
Find my haven as God may have planned.

——∘∘○─◉─○∘∘——

11

A DIALOGUE WITH THE CREATOR

O merciful Lord,
Why my longing for you
Drags me further away to
Turn me a stranger to myself.
Neither I reach you,
Nor get to know myself.
As it be not enough,
To top it You play
Hide and seek with me.
But O lord, in growing taller,
Cunningly wiser and clever,
Child frustrated parted me long ago.
In being always in rush to living my will,
Lured to climbing unending
Non-existing steps to the top,
At the end I discover
Thoroughly fatigued,
I have reached nowhere...

Tell me O lord,
Having landed at where I am,
How do I play hide and seek with you
Minus the child in me?
Where do I get the energy to play to
Run around tireless inspired?
Hiding all over yet always getting caught.
It drenches me sweating all over tired though
Does fill me with joy dripping out from head to toe.

I am aware in being different now.
Actually all together different though
I do miss the child occasionally within.
But in being tied to gain and loss always,
I am centered in gain dread losses.
Let me tell Lord, though it's no secret to you;
Even in my prayers I dream to gain.
If I sensed it a waste, even thought of it
Would not enter my mind.

O Lord, to seeking I have lived and
Breathe to seek.
Never could learn there is more to seeking than
Eyes have grown to seeing.
I realize lord in realizing as
Sun is about to set that
It's not the eyes that see
But only when the vision is blessed.

12

LETS COOL DOWN

Lets cool down.
Lets agree we have option none.
Lets cool down to the World.
As well cool down the world in us to
Help World cool us down.
Let us pull down its
vertically rising temperature.
Let us step down its
Horizontal fueling that
Add flame to rise further.
Lets for a change live cool to
Bridging out all gaps that
Persisting endless as if
On an auto mode to
Widen gap all over.
Distancing heart from the mind.
Mind squeezing heart constant
Distancing mind from mind.

Differences in rise add
ugliness to stink that
Radically impacting climatic order.
Chaotically polluting the sky all over.
As well the earth, water and air.
Contaminating food to further goal to
Poisoning heart, poisoning mind.
Throwing open the gate to mass annihilation.
Devil ridden multiplying earth's sufferings.
Motherhood impaired beyond repair.

Mountains denuded.
Greenery burnt.
Vegetation insanely burnt.
Life in the wild rampant slaughtered,
Wilderness left to stand stark naked.
Dried up barren of its wild beauty.
Hunger reining havoc.
Horror multiplying endless.
Insanity grown epidemic.
Killing stretched to
being a fashionable sport that
Stretch to hit a new horizon beyond hell.

Doors and windows to sanity broken down.
Its dwelling burnt out.
Pray, let us stand back for a change to
Witness it reeled out how
Act mounted over act is put to action.
If it's a glory to rejoice; Let's celebrate our doom?

Shackled and weather beaten
Humanity torn into shreds
Been made dumb fear stricken.
Left to rust and age it has grown fragile.
Let us for a change look back to
Retrace path to get back home.

13

MAKING OF A MEMORIAL

Yes, it's going to be a memorial day,
Memorial for sure of glamour, of euphoria,
Of hope and promises.
Of doubt and apprehension.
Of tricks of trade.
Of love and hate.
Of victory and defeat.
Of success and failure that
Swim past fast into common void.
Washed off the dream spelt that weave
Future into present to
soothingly flow flooded for a change yet,
carefully keeping banks intact soaked up in joy to
Rounding up all sharp corners smooth.
The Sun set to rise in its
Full glamor and brilliance to
Lighten all hearts.
The child within awakened afresh would
wear sparkle that sparkles heart in the eyes.

Centered in all new toys
it would have it all that
rings and runs,
sings and dance,
all at flick of a finger.

Wrinkled out weather beaten faces
lived through vagaries of life,
living on venom soaked words that
Honey dipped sweeten to let
Lies shine forth better than truth.
Wait, wait, wait they tell
Wait, wait, wait they yell.
So what if wait appear eternally stretched?
Must not one pay
For emergence of dawn to
Painting life in choicest color?
Wherein dream, they assure shall
Thrive alive full throttled!

Yes, night shall end.
It would for sure.
It's been so ever since
Life breathed its first.
Witnessed through millennia
Over and over.
Life has been tuned to its rhythm.
Sometime unbearably rough.

At times it's been all music.
But then the next is a blast.
It revolves in a cycle in an
Unpredictable rhythm.
Darkness and light though
Differ in nature are but one in being
Twin sides of a coin.
In that wind blows
Propelled by forces unknown.
It may blow to cool down heat.
At the next it may a volcanic burst
Lava flowing all over.
It may churn the sea upside down
Wherein roaring waves would rise to
flooding all over....
Drowning each soul along its cage.
Wherein villainous whirls tear out silence
into countless pieces.
The devil let loose
churn and burn the spirit to
Let horror rise hell bent.

Life has horror soaked witnessed it all
Over and over through millennia and
Hence the wise in their wisdom live it all
In acceptance of destiny that time strikes
As may heaven choose to blow.

Pushed into the pool of promises,
Wrapped dry to hold it in hope;
Horizon sniggers at it in wild contempt.
Sky disgusted shuts off eyes in shame.
Yet, hardened and cracked inside out.
Life never cease to plough its field.
Head tilted frequent heavenwards
Begins to see the truth in the false
In hovering clouds.
Know for sure it shall bring not rain.
Yet, barring pinning hope what
Choice life has to cling?

Then sudden rise a mighty glow over horizon.
Could it be God-incarnate glows?
Finally perhaps to end all curse on the wait,
To tear apart darkness. Could it really be true?
If it truly be, it makes it a memorial to live in heart
Wherein faith in heaven is endorsed at last!
Yet apprehension coiled up cling still
Head being held in python's jaw.
Eyes coaxed to open up to seeing it fresh to
Let nerves feel the difference heart strikes.
Yes, its a concert of thousand
strings struck together that
Rise and fall in rhythm sweetness soaked to
Reshaping hope long last lost into oblivion....

If it all be true, devoid of that
Time's divide played in the past,
Let it be the Sun rise to waking up heart to
Shake up and choke of all horror at source to
Burying all yesterdays, from its beginning till date.
All put together to breathe fair and free in
Dawn's glory freshly gathered and the rest
All tidbits scattered be casted
new in fresh human mold
Burying for good all that be bitter to let
Heart's glory reach out heaven's door to
Strike an era never ever lived nor known
Wherein future is drawn into present
Shaping out dreams to life
Casting and recasting it into
Virtue's dynamics constant to
Rise above that time strikes harsh.
To let humanity sparkle in its eternal glow,
Even to rope in all devils to sharing dreams
Just as Creator may have in creating dreamt!

14

ELECTION

It is on, the fever, the mania, the chase
With bundle and bundles of truth clad lies
Blared rampant rent air in multicolor, multi tune
Blown out fly all over tearing sky apart that
Blend perfect with air to contaminate further that
Hypocrisy collective permeate
All over the Country. Polluting at large-
Its land, its air, its sky that
Its inmates made to breathe in heart and mind.
It perpetuate day in and day out.
Have perpetuated years rolled into years.
Decades into decades.
So much so that child born
Grown old way before age would strike wrinkles...
Accelerated forces of change defy life force
Intensifying darkness to grow constant darker.

And the joke of joke, loud mouth collective
Rain promises of golden era in
wait round the corner that
exercising the right choice
Can be had for asking...
Each mouth blare out to be the choice with
Their shady tainted past bears it all.
Name it and it has it.

Election over promises vanish.
Faster than vanishing ink on paper.

Yes, that rise must fall is the law eternal,
But for those blown mighty, risen too smart and half,
Easily outmaneuver it all to
Turn and twist it into their favor but
The meek and simple, credulous god fearing soul,
It visibly shatters faith held to
Bear the pang of fathomless wait?

Time accumulated filth of years
Get flung rampant names calling grow filthy
Surpassing civil limits.
Rivalry intense, inflict insults spread over public that
Only add injuries intensifying agony to
Make people suffer that none care...

The helpless mother of all mother, the mother earth
Dumbfounded lost, meekly gazes at the sky
For a heavenly spark of mercy amongst stars that
May blow it all to ending dark night.
Pinning hope as much on heavenly body to
Believe someday Sun would rise different to
Burn out insanity
In the darkened crevices of human brain to
Relish freedom as well to dream free that
Heart happily clings to, yet, she knows the
Truth of truth; It's a wishful hope.
Just as its been through decades, all a waste to
Searching the needle in the hay stack
At dead of night....

Mother Earth knows, like all unfortunate mothers
Choice to be none, never had any.
Witnessed through millennia
Over and over again. Choice if any been to
Accept the fait-accompli.
Life force gripped constant in death's claw
Grow stronger each moment yet,
Tragedy of tragedy is:
It keep senses wide awake to live through it
A l i v e.

15

JOURNEY NOT BEGUN

I claim authority over none
Let alone on anything,
Even onto myself.
Governing that govern is a battle that
One knows not how one must fight?
The survival instinct centered at the core
Clouds mind and blur out vision.
In it all whirl past so fast that
It flows constant right under my nose.
It throws me to wonder whether that
Jump and bounce and toss me
Up and down like a ball is-
Heaven pushing me downwards or
Mother earth holing up to saving my soul?

II

At times I wonder without being cynical,
Shame set aside, if truly I am in being
Held on to a base that holds me or been
Randomly picked to being myself?
Never knowing who the hell may I be that
Surfaced on this earth and why?
Wonder if I ever loved my parents, my
Brothers and sisters, and friends and
The soil I claim to belong to and love or
Its been all so far a stage work to
Reflect in all to matching it?

III

Knowingly well all along that I am not...
What perplexes measure beyond is;
Which must truly be me midst
Many I stage at convenience dictate?
Wherein I flow along fairly at ease
Free of remorse and shame safely
Flung onto time to blow it as may it wish.

IV.

Who may then I must be
Midst all upheaval but me?
Being the focal point that
History relates and reflects over of
Wars, bloodshed, cunning and deceit of
Kings and emperors, mutiny and revolts.
Of great temples and mosques,
Churches and palaces and forts,
Prophets and Saviors,
Saints and Satan that I see in me.
Together split me into many on stage that
Cling in me like skin to the bone or as
Bone to skin and many including that
Erupt unscheduled at will.
Act and react perplexingly
In multiple ways, so much so that
Held me rock like turns into quicksand.

V.

But then what makes me sail along
Midst all that add, subtract, multiply,
Regardless of all I speculate that
Over millennia lived through
Drowned me into great big void that have
Always pronounced abrupt my journey's end?
And yet intriguingly casted and re-casted
Repeatedly over and over,
Such strange sensation flood into veins that
Bursts forth invisibly to reflect that
Though millennia over life been made to
Route through many paths,
Man has yet to learn to crown life it deserves.

16

TO BE ISN'T REALLY TO BEING!

It's been what it is that
I have lived
Birth after birth
Persisted eternally
Over and over
Within closed doors to-
To be into being...
Courage did stand mighty to
Live it all unfazed.
Be it cyclone, tornado or tsunami
Just as a banyan tree
Takes all the beatings to
Standing tall in obstinate denial
Holds its ground unshaken.

At every Sun rise
Path appear strange
As been ever.
Rough, circuitous
Frightfully tricky and slippery.
Never ending that
bind and bend at will that
Drop sudden unwarned
deep down the abyss.
Worse than the game of ladder
Children play.
Reverses stretch endless to
Never reaching nowhere.... and
What is - may what it be,
Change color faster than chameleon
Random in quick succession in
Multicolored, multi shape, multi design.
Delude to varying degrees.
Pile up questions that
Revolve constant around its axis perplexing
In countless ways.
Where sun sets frequent than rise.

How on earth does one guard against
That be dark in the light?
As against even a faint glow
Let sail through the darkest night
Even though seen be not actually the seen.
Hence I am tossed perennially
Between is and isn't,
In being and being not.
Desperate I keep pinching hard into flesh to
Feel if I am still alive....

Guess, blessed are those
Who have joyfully arrived.
I know I have not, hence
Still wandering homeless.
Let the stranger within keep playing with itself
Despite that rise like a bright star to lead path.
I am kicked hard to gather that
Merely to be isn't really to being.
There is more and more and yet endlessly more
Before journey may truly commence to hitting light.

17

WELCOMING NEW YEAR

Born onto new wings with
fresh woven hopes,
all dressed up to bid farewell to the old
earth and sky scrubbed clean bright to
Ending all that was old
to Welcoming the New.
Sun dressed anew groom like riding over
ageless darkness to let
Horizon glow in heavenly hue.
Temples crowded to the brim,
Jam packed with aspirations and hopes.
Blend together culminate in prayers that
Echo through Conch blown loud to
Embracing the new to
Bury old deep down the abyss to
Let rivers flow heart and mind
Thoroughly cleansed flow
Vibrating life as a whole to
Embracing the sea.

But alas! as the Sun strikes midday
Coolness vanished it scorches and burn,
The euphoria erupt in the built up zeal that
Had risen sudden high into sky
Fell flat as zeal leaked out to
Fall back as easy onto
age old carved mold to
Revolve around old grooves,
churning misery to life that merrily
Nip spirit risen in the bud..
Instinct push birds to
fall back onto their old wings.
Life recedes to trace back old path.
Horizon back to wearing its gloom.
The Sun onto its monotonous course.
And men onto their old ways
perennially playing hide and seek.
Played ages through...

Welcoming the New Year
did rise with a bang to
end in a whimper.

18

WHAT WOULD YOU DO?

What would you do?
what may any one do?
Leave alone me with
all my pretended
near perfected perfection
Guard round the clock.
It all stayed pretty until
Secrets locked burst open and
The cat jumped out of hiding that
Sparked up bolts out of blue to explode.
Debris flying all over.
From and without that
Gushed forth from all sides
tearing apart all protective base to shreds.

A JOURNEY WITHIN

Choked and heckled,
caught in the vortex in being
forced down the throat,
Survival instinct
fights desperate to breathe.
It only furthers
burst of misery in
luring vultures to devour
life's remains in the dream...

Looking back and
Looking at the lost within,
I fall flat hanging onto void.
Earth gripped me not,
neither sky let hang on to it.
I understand and
understand it well now as
It dawns loud and clear with
Pros and cons of all
gained and lost beyond,
wherein mind is
purged out clean.
I surrender and
surrender joy burst
to get beyond time's hold.
Past present future thrown to bin,
I step out cleansed of all inflict in
loss and gain, victory and defeat.
d i s r o b e d f u l l.

Ratnakar was lost in Valmiki.
Breathing free I explode into laugh.
laughing at it all, expanded beyond
I never knew I was capable of.

Gratitude drenched,
freed of shackles of time wherein
desire breeds its net.

I dive blindfold into unknown
into its dark mountainous waves
and lo! rise back cradled blessed.
Basking in heaven's eternal warmth,
I sleep and sleep fully awake
rocked in love's oozing waves and
as a child I cozily sleep and sleep
in its warm eternal embrace
breathing free beyond life and death.

(Ratnakar was a notorious dacoit who looted and killed
people merciless to take care of his family with the loot.
When he learnt no one in the family agreed to share his
sin, he was greatly perturbed and to atone his sin he
did severe penance as guided by celestial Sage Narad.
It was so severe that he was totally unaware of termite
built structure over and around him. He emerged as
sage Valmiki who wrote Ramayan, an Hindu Epic that
portrays the life of Lord Ram.)

19

I VOTED FOR WAR

In being the world that frustratingly
grown insane in me,
threw me to war in
most unpropitious manner.
I gathered it's nothing new,
neither ever been...

I may be on a journey to peace that
I know nothing of except
It stands opposite to that
I am made to live with.
Its the opposite that I suffer
wherein peace is a mere abstraction.
It burns my head in rage.
Palm rise to cooling it and
Heart stands lost in being a dumb
Witness to it all.

It can't bear the weight of
Albatross around its neck.
Standing tall within conclude:
Peace can never be had for asking.
And one can't wander through life
pursuing a pathless path.

Hence I am carried away
in my zeal to earning peace even if
it costs me war. I am aware
nothing ever comes free and
Peace has visibly a price that's
Far beyond control of
Mighty market forces.
No term secures it and
Its far beyond calculation.
Pay full or like an eel
it slips out of hand even
before one may realize.

The tragedy it strikes is
it being never on sale yet
bears a price which works out to be
far above the ordinary in being rare.
Far greater than a rare diamond or
an oasis in a cruel desert, or
regaining love lost, or
even that may dare to snatch life
back from the clutches of death.
Its unaided lone venture to
Climbing mount Everest
warring constant with own self to
Uphold dying spirit, yet
grip keep slip away...
Hence I guess,
it has to be carved out
with tools of war to let
phoenix keep rise from
its ashes.

Meaning is not always meant, neither
Mere knowing is knowledge nor
Knowledge wisdom to strengthen heart,
Neither definition is the defined as
Name may be to being.
Its far more complex
A mystery wrapped up
In endless layers that
In description meaning is lost.
As if it never had its origin in the creation.
Beside merely fantasizing dream
Shall never lure lions at great
Temple door to roar.

Hence the conclusion
Sets me to warring to
Earning peace.
Even it be mere a glimpse at end that
Graveyard sparks....
Even it be for name sake.
It bears its lure rest in abstraction to
Perpetuate living life warring
Totally dried out of love to earning
Peace.

20

IN LIVING THE WORLD WITHOUT BEING WORLDLY

Friends and foes allege alike
I am a dud who knows not nothing.
Can't even tell east from west
Nor moon from the sun,
So much so even left from right.
Oh! How I would give my right eye for
It to be true to being blessed.
Let the whole world scream against me
tearing out its lungs and heart calling me dud or
as they may wish calling me names.
I would rejoice in being filled with joy to the brim.
Against all odds that sprinkle salt on wound,
I would savor the salt along the wound.
I bet, It would be more tastier than
Adding tons of spices to make life relish living.

Living its day and night regardless of plane,
In that all undulations merge to becoming of me,
Just as riding a giant wheel take me to the top and
bring me down at a speed; Up and down joyfully
Merged become one in me.
I levitate free to the peak floating down at ease.
Swing along the concert life plays
on divine instruments.
Never knew nor ever seen or could imagine it being
played with such divine skill, it transported me to
a plane soaked in thrilling joy that
Made me dripping wet inside out.
Oh, one may know it only floating in its rhythm.
It evaporated all my earthly rumblings.
It struck out discord to vanish nonexistent.
I was turned into a song floating in air to its rhythm.
How I wish to wishing nothing in
being drowned in it for ever.
Heaven only knows to the plane it elevated me ;
Wherein world and worldly merged
Washed of clean of all duality within.

21

HIDE AND SEEK

Either its flood or famine
You push me into that
It's always been.
connected as fast disconnected.
It's the way I am played
hide and seek.
I mind not and
I labor hard,
Have always labored
through and through to get to
the Sun never to set in me
nor Moon to ever wane.
So that in playing your game
I glow with the Sun,
Shining cool with moon to
Carry all your intrigues to
Playing hide and seek with its
Repeated cast and recast of rules.
With its joys of sufferings.

Just as Sun scorches the earth
Cracking face merciless and
Just when its driven
Onto the verge of collapse,
Clouds burst out to
Turn earth glow greener and richer.
Yet, game I am played with
endlessly measure my
perpetually starved eyes that
Stay ever stretched
Set on to vacant sky for
A glimpse of Your shadow
In the clouds to burst forth to
Drench me deep.
Penetrated void to
Glow green in being one
With the mother earth.
My gratitude dripping wet,
My parched tongue craving
Greedily lick each precious drop to
Quenching age old thirst
As never before....

But You keep me
Savagely engaged to
Keep my endless wait to
End never....
I know, have known it
Over and over
Millennia through
Playing your games Your way.
Conforming to your terms,
Each breath neatly
woven incomprehensibly
into intrigue yet
Abundantly joy filled.
Do what You may.
I would play it not in
Any other way than
You make me play to suffer.
I know You play games to
keep me blessed.

22

WHAT IS, IS WHAT IS….

I sure don't claim to know this world.
Though ever since time began,
It has ground me to gather
Right and wrong,
Right in the wrong and
Wrong in right.
Together good, bad, evil, worse.
Living it in breath to measure my path
Paying toll through and through
Onto all channels traversed that did
Sparked bright to start with but soon
Grew strangely dark despite
Sky glowing still bright
In the glow of Sun,
The Moon and the stars to
Light up this glorious planets.

Sky hovering over followed suit.
Darkened my horizon ceaseless.
To stay on to path, my eyes strained to
See if there be even a faint silver line to
hold back that shattered in being
Reached nowhere...

As in the gathered tidbits
Accounted for it not,
Man and the world grew in me still
Along all that been, looked clear,
Even in the darkened gleam of sunset.
With all the intrigue clinging still
Beyond grasp, wherein time in raze
Bursts forth in dreadful rhythm
Unceremoniously
blew me off the course,
Tearing apart my flow
At a mere touch of a glance.
Dumped me merciless
at middle of nowhere.
Never to reach nowhere.

Thrown lost top to toe,
Carrying all gathered
Through and through that
Neither can be borne nor thrown.
Yet, load mounted set aside
World grew heavier still within.
It threw me off guard to wonder,
If the light flickered within were
The curses rubbed ruthless or
Blessings to seeing beyond to see,
what is, is what is, is what is!!!

23

MY LOVE

Let me tell I love you in being that you are in me;
just as soft breeze feels soaked in moon's beam,
just as moon beam feel dancing on cool sea waves,
just as peace reins quiet in country side,
just as it feels lazily lying on green grass care free
untouched by thought, untouched by desire
In being fully awakened to dawn wherein
inner and outer merge in harmony
Inseparably become one.

Have loved spark of your creativeness
spark out in me that glows in my cravings to
sing of its oozing sweetness.
But words being words fail to match the ineffable.
In that heart fails to match its rhythm
Having no means to express.
just as a blind would fail to tell
The color of its mother's milk.
All that be blunt pierce into

my failings hard yet, it hurts not,
An uncanny gift blessed to
Bear all blows that holds me intact still to
standing tall in that all your reflects glow.

Yes, I love you without being tied to any boundary.
Neither to any mission, nor a destination nor
Ever wish it to be defined, nor let any element to
Striking any bond that translates me into
Its pain and pleasure to keep
Pushing me back and forth to that
I have severed ties for ever.
No, it stands solitary alone,
On its own resting at none,
sailing free independent,
unconcerned of destination.
It borrows not wings to fly in being blessed;
Wingless it flies at will, free of craving, free of desire.
Nameless in its wholeness that shines forth in moon,
Absorbed in that the sun reflects
to absorbing all heart;
Breaks open all dark chambers of mind to
Setting it free to let joy blissfully flow
Eternally glowing in its spread out glory.

24

ENDGAME

What is it that reflects
Beyond words barring a certainty
Unavoidable,
A fact unalterable,
Neither more, nor less.
Immutable.
Beyond scope of bargain.
A Truth,
Wherein darkness dissolves
Beyond itself.

A drama wherein characters
Eternally emerge and vanish,
Roll in to act,
Good, bad, evil,
Heroes and villains,
Tyrants and saints,
As well lesser beings,
Lives below living,
And those inflict sufferings,

And those voices
Bursts forth,
For and against,
And those remain silent,
To reflect and define
Words for words,
Words against words,
Words into words,
Pain, joy, sorrow,
Divided into acts,
Action, reaction, responses,
Good, bad, evil,
Merge to be total
Led by pathless path
Into bottomless womb
wherein destiny
Translated into destination
Eternally upholds continuity....

Its so simple.
Stars fall from heaven and
Disappears into thin air
Merged into elements,
In time
All acts end,
Clock stops,
Curtain is downed on
Beginning and end.
In that time's reflect all
Merge into itself.

25

OH! HOW I WISH

Oh! how I wish to
Flying free at will.
In being the wind to
Flying shackles free,
High above stars
Twinkling within.
Even though it be
A mere drop to soothe
Parched out throat....
I am aware,
The very moment
Eternity compressed
Lead to comprehending
The eternal,
Wherein existence in chain
Secures release to flowing free.

joy drenched-
Nay, in being the joy
To laugh and cry.
Swim, dive, float, fly.
Absorbed beyond
Grasp of earthly sense that
Time and space govern.

26

ENDING CLEAN MY WANDERINGS

Who would know what it is
That hold me tall and the very next
Throws me to melt into darkness.
Been running mad over lost ever since.
Darkness reining over
Merrily shut me in making sure
No doors at sight
Tempts me to knock...

Spirit dampened sees the world too big
That grow tiny sudden to denying me space.
In being tossed constant duality seized,
Been looking for the beginning in the end to
See through all perceived
To rejoining heart to
My own little world.

I venture to
Trace back left out dreamt.
But then world
Grown crowded has
Eroded all sign of it,
Leaving me no room to
Beginning afresh.

Wandering aimless into the wilderness,
I look for a leeway to contain me whole.
But against that surface rampant
Defy forthright, pronounce loud that
Echoes in me "boat missed is
Missed forever."

With heavy heart I return to
Recreate flavor of loneliness within,
I break down doors and windows that
Resist breeze to flowing free and fresh.
To let my heart sing all over again in being
The flow of rhythm to matching its tune.

Solitude reining loud strikes to let
Life breathe free filled in cheers.
Spreading out greenery to my little old world.
In being home finally ending clean my wanderings.

27

I AM NOT SIGNED OUT YET….

I am not signed out yet.
I still look at all my mail without reading.
That I wish to as much as I don't, for
I know it would repeat carrying stench of air
Been blowing across my heaven and earth
With its nauseating stink.
Though I care little yet,
Can't bear its stench that penetrate
Far deeper than sense grown immune can block.
Though all other blows reaching me lose its impact.
As it is, pain rising beyond a point grow anesthetic.

Then again dead can't be made to breathe into
Your intricate fancies that
You trade at will taking me to be.
I am aware of all your make up
To project me dead as much you would wish to.
Let me tell, I aren't. Neither grown myopic.
Nor inert though my senses have
Grown immune to all your stings.

Yet, fully alive with its
Million eyes to feel the world.
Bring in something more lethal for
The effect you crave for.
Arrows tried so far have achieved you
Little to blow out my flicker. I know
It would pave your path easy further.
As much to ease out parting pretension free.
It would let you flow merrily along your fancies to
Exploring new pastures that
You barely bear to wait.

O I am sick and tired of all your
Hide and seek game.
I here and now flush you out of my head
Even if it leads to
Lighting my candle at both ends.
It would for a change
Let night rejoice glowing bright
To light me up in its glow.

I have known all your tricks that
You play which no matter how I look at it.
It sticks ugly on you all over that
Put to action magnify further.
I am aware of all your
Venom soaked arrows you
Clandestinely hid in your coffer that
Act to your will, shoot to kill.

In that you Beat chameleon in changing color
Without as much a flicker of shame.

Let it flow onto you loud and clear that
I have grounded all concern
Grinding past dust to
Breaking ties beyond all lures.
Woman, you are not, much though
You may claim worthy of my concern.
I have no gears to change,
Neither any ware to trade.
I am in being I am.
Charged mighty to bear all blows
To bearing you out at ease.

All being finite, temporary, brief,
You go your way, leaving me to mine.
Let your indulgence multiply your senses mighty to
Carrying you on to new height to fall.
Woman, I need not forgive you for
You would seek it in time when bell rings.
I for me, set you free to
Trade your ware free to merit your desire.

28

IN BEING ME

I do not breathe but
Its the breath that
breathes me in and out.
Often lifeless and stale that
Mechanically act in
Most disconcerted rhythm,
Flowing through choked channels
That flow not wherein
Life glows to sparkle.

I love the parrot sure but
Only it being a parrot.
As in the wild.
Can not when
Its taught to sing of love.
I dread dead words that's
Pasted on to look smart.

That appear just as a
Weather bitten sign board
Stands in the wild that
One knows not what to make of it.
So much so even wilderness would
Despise it sing of love.

In being I am, and not that
Blown into me to being and
In that to let love to flow out as
Parrot made to sing.
No, I need flow from
Up above mountain top to
Being I am.
In being whole.

In that ice melts to its warmth.
Oozes out in rhythm to let life dance.
To sing that heart sings into heart drenched
Exalted in its tune to the pore.
It breathes its aroma to floating in air,
Carrying the sky together in to trance.
Universe as a whole wrapped in its embrace
Locked in to being one in love's hold.

29

I AM AWARE

I am aware to being the crowd.
As well of the crowd to
Carrying the crowd.
Marching along with it, though
It may look different. yet
The whole crowd is in me
At large running around,
Within and out.
In being it, I am its world.
Pain and sorrow, pleasures and joys.
In living it, time consumes me in its net.
It breathes in its rise and fall in sustaining me and
I dare to bear it alone with the crowd within, though
Shamefully be ignorant of that percolates.
Be it legitimate, illegitimate that move along all
Merged in the urge to live.

Living it on war path that
Strike time and again to
Being the end cry of the wild in being
Pulled and pushed unsure of where it all began;
Ignored through and through since time began.
In not being reckoned to despite all hue and cry.
A silent witness to bearing the brunt
Pronounced through timelessness,
Screaming it out in the wilderness within

30

WALKING THROUGH FROZEN SAND DUNES

I am lost walking through
The vast frozen sand dunes.
Dumbfounded lost
Under the full moon up above
Soothingly glowing bright.
I have landed dazed
At the cross road of chaos
Having nowhere to turn to.
Shadows chase
Playing hide and seek.
Run along and out run
Every now and then.
Jackals and wolves howling
Blowing heart full throated.
And I, being the lone world all alone,
Stare at the frozen sand inside out.

Envy the glorious full moon shining above that
Casts in me mercifully the promise of
Golden Sun at the strike of dawn.
Whispering sweet when wait ends,
One finds the path to get back home.

In landing at all cross road of chaos I have had
Such whispers sweetly often ringed in my ears.
It were words, sweet words, promising words yet
Never more than words as all words are.
Have known of all hollow words by sound that
Never bridged in to take me across...and
I am as ever been alone;
Fear soaked and terror drenched carrying
A lone lost world within in being along
The echo of strange howling at the dead of night.
Directionless, motionless, standing dumb
Midst frozen sand dunes stretched endless.
Dragging past into present into projecting future that
Holds in me over the parched land stretch.
Wherein dread echoes full throated howling
Along the wolves and jackals and everything strange.
Oh! I am surrounded by
jackals and wolves all around...within and out.

As eyes set at nowhere stretch beyond;
Hands rise on its own in prayer in seeing within
The showering glory spread all over.
Awakened I melt in to shame
In being an alien to the
Soothing beams of full moon soaked in divine silence.
Wherein divine sparkled midst
Millions of twinkling stars that
Even the desert woken up to rejoice drenched in
Divine glory dripping far up from above.
It was a celebration. My victory over myself,
While merciless cold wind blew hard still
Over frozen sand dunes that
Freeze me still in being thrown out of myself.
I am done to that stretched me into terror.
Frail hope no longer frail holds me far above to
Being the Sun to light up world within
waking up dead to rise in spite of itself!

31

AS IT ROLLS AWAY

Years have rolled away in the flow of time and
In being dumb spectator we been flowing along
Witnessing it all tied up into that fancy holds.
Sometime jolted, at times restless and helpless yet,
Most of the time that grow indifferent in time to
Flowing away with the current hardly knowing
Where to, until need to know strikes no more;
Just as a fallen leaf blown in the wind ever need.
None know though few dare, dive deep to figure,
Soon surface empty handed with none to share.
Yet, when I pause to look within to see get lost.
Who is it flowing away to where, why and to what?
Answer surface none no matter
how deep I dig or dive,
Wherein I witness questions that riddle
Only breed questions faster than I can
Hardly cope to finding any answer.

How in hell one may unriddle it all to breathe free?
Alas, all effort grow complex wound up within
confound and confuse that lead to conclude;
Freedom ought be a myth wherein hope perpetuate.
Life is pushed to battle constant
Far more within than out.
Never knowing why or what,
Neither ever reaching the summit.

32

TO BEING LIGHT TO ONESELF

It's been what it is that
I have lived dying many deaths
A single life could afford and yet,
Have persisted over and over
Despite locked within to
Breathing under closed door
To be into being...

Courage did not let down to
Living it all unfazed.
Be it cyclone, tornado,
Or tsunami,
Just as banyan tree
Takes all beatings yet
Holds its ground
Standing tall unmoved.

A JOURNEY WITHIN

At every Sun rise path ahead
Appear strange as ever.
Rough, circuitous.
Frightfully tricky, slippery.
Never ending stretched endless
That bind and bend at will.
Drop sudden deep
Down into abyss.
Worse than the game of ladder.
Wherein rise and reverses though be
But endless never.
Chance does hit to lead to
Get to the peak.
But treading the path of lure
End never neither lead to any
Meaningful end despite dying
Over and over wrapped in its
Cumulative inflict with its endless
Recurrence of pain and sorrow.

What is it? May what it be,
Change color faster in quick succession
In multicolor, multi shape,
Multi design that delude easy
In varying degree that perplex
In countless ways revolving endless
Around its own axis wherein
Sun sets frequent....

Hell, how does one guard against
That grow dark in the light?
Even a faint glow
Spark up courage to sail through
The darkest night even though
Seen actually be not the seen.
Hence I am tossed between
Is and isn't.
In being and being not,
Desperate keep pinching
Hard into flesh to sense
Spark of life....

I guess, blessed one are those
Who have joyfully arrived.
I know and fully aware that
I have not and hence
Wander homeless to
Let the stranger fool itself.

Kicked hard shaken and jolted
Gather in the end that
Merely to be isn't
Really to being.
There is far more
That stretch endless before
A traveler hits to being
The light on to himself.

33

IN THAT I REVOLVE ROUND AND ROUND

I claim no authority over anything.
Let alone on anything, even on myself for
In governing that govern,
The survival instinct overworked often splits to
Clouding mind and blurring vision that
Whirl past fast constant under my nose
Throwing me to wonder whether that
jump and bounce strange tossing
me up and down been
The heaven pushing me downwards or
Mother earth holding me up to saving my soul?

At times I wonder without being cynical,
Shamelessly perhaps to setting aside shame if
I truly belonged to my parents or I
Strayed thrown to being myself?

It leads me to wonder who the hell may I be?
Did I ever actually grew up to love my parents?
Brothers and sisters, my friends?
The soil I claim to love that
I have sworn convincing myself to belong to, or
Its been all a stage work to
Reflect in them my sense of belonging
Knowingly all along I am not?
What perplexes measure beyond is;
Which must truly be me midst
Many staged almost truthfully yet,
At convenience dictate that
I follow and flow flowing fairly at ease
Free of either remorse or burdened with shame that
Flung over on to time to blow it as may it wish.

Who may then be in midst of all upheaval but me that
History meticulously relates and reflects
Of wars, bloodshed, cunning and deceit of
Kings and emperors, mutiny and war,
Of great temples and mosques and churches,
Palaces and forts, of Saints and Satan that
I see in me together it all though no way
I would wish to house all in me along past,
Present or future in being
Disgusted, shaken and frightened
Reflected of that swim in my eyes.

Heaven may know why it all
Cling to me like skin to the bone to
Wonder if I am only bone to the skin or
As be flesh to bone or both or still many that
Erupt sudden unscheduled,
Act and react at will in multiple ways within
Leaving me densely perplexed,
So much so the ground that held me rock like solid
Turns into quick sand sudden totally unwarned

But then what makes me still sail along
Midst that add, subtract, multiply,
Regardless of all I speculate that
Over millennia lived through
Drown me lost into great big void that
Pronounce all sudden journey's end?
And yet intriguingly cast strange sensation that
Bursts forth invisibly to reflect that
Though millennia over life been made to
Route through many paths,
Man mighty has yet to gather its root to crown life!!!

34

IN WHAT I SEE

I see, its the matter of what I see,
But what I see I understand not;
How a single phenomena multiplying
May rest on my choice to
Seeing the sun as sun,
Moon as moon and
All in the name spread over
Pronounced in me?
Repeatedly over time and again to
Be all as all in that
None and nothing left out.
But in me it is not all that's seen,
(As if mere seen were to be the known.)
And then again not to everywhere I have been.
Neither I can nor can be the seen in the unseen.
How would I see the unseen to be
No different than it actually be?
In response to that I act and react to head to
Seeing lies as lies and fact as fact.

Knowing as known and known be that -
That I may claim to be the truth; That
Appear dressed in multicolor
Overlapping wild over the other that
One can't see the one in many in its
Multidimensional reflect that perplex and
Confuse to being many in one or
In being one in many?
O hell! I am confusion burst to
Confusing the world in and about me to
Being the unseen in the seen.
It dawns in me that mere
Seeing is hardly the seen;
As mere to be is not to being and
Neither acting god can ever be the God.
I begin understanding it just as
Mere skin isn't the whole wherein
Truth is held just as belief in the believed.

I see, feeling it at the end that
Finally appear in me as what I see midst
Thousand and one unseen that
I know not what to make - head or tail
That I am held mighty to being by the unseen
In being the world wherein
Dreams weave desire dare
Flying onto unknown
Devoid of wings!

35

BURNT TOAST

It's not always simple to
Doing things right that
Meets all eyes.
As to being simple may mean
Chewing burnt toast with a grin
Under high voltage that burns both
Toaster as well the toast.

In being what it be.
Bad can be only bad, or
May it be good to some eyes as
Angle of vision may determine to
Pronounce it as may sense preside.
But in the eyes of sealed lips,
Bad is bad be it pronounced or not
As bad can be that throws
Life to tantrum yet induced to
Munching silently the served coolly
Wearing a face befitting to survive
Storm blown tide that beat

Merciless rough on to shore that
Toss it over to frightening height only to
As ruthlessly dump it on the melting lap of
Lightening and thunder...

Pronounced can't be quietened by
Noble wish or prayer.
In being as it turns out to be,
The perpetuating stink of aftermath
Even pigs decline to relish...

Sky painted dark all over
Stretched layers over layers;
None to bother how and why
Toaster was burnt.
What is eyed upon is toast that
burnt black look bleak as future.
Hence toaster at this stage a namesake a
Reference, neither here nor there.
At least for time being till hunger persists.
None dare to dig at the source.
None dare tell its dawn or dusk.
As darkness thicken still darker...
But then toast burnt is a burnt toast that
Crumbles into ash.
Wind carries it across land.

And then done is done
Repeatedly over to
Keeping the flame alive
For the posterity to continue with
Ongoing war of prejudice and injustice....

Like the poor little girl
While combing her hair
Breaks mirror slipped out of hand.
Lo the thud, promptly throws
House into raze against
poor girl's crime.
All eyes centered on great mirror.
None at the girl if she is hurt.
Storm over, little girl wonders
How come voice never rise
against wreckage spread
that routinely piled up
higher and higher.
Blood dripping all over of slaughter.
parched land starved of water
Bathing in blood!
Yet, mirror broken razes a storm and
Burnt toast is coolly chewed,
While blood flowing across the land.
All in the name of justice.

Little girl would soon
Get over her innocence to
Join the band.
Spirit of vengeance simmer multiplying
Defining justice from a new angle.
Land would perpetuate to
Starve of water.
It would continue bathing in blood.
Let wreckage pile up.
Voltage must be kept high.
Let it keep burning out both
Toaster and the toast...

Like it or not,
Onlookers, bystander shall
Live on leftover ashes of the burnt to
Face carved out destiny even
before destiny
Pronounce its course.
While Man risen to its
New found wisdom
Be it black, blue, red,
hit end far ahead of it to
Strike a beginning as may its
Wisdom blindly spell.

36

KNOW NOT WHAT...
DREAM OR REAL

Know not what that scratches,
Stirs and corrodes within that
Clueless stretch beyond the
Field of reason that
Pleasantly choke to breathlessness.
Something far yet near but invisible that
Strangely feels visible as
Cool breeze on face feels at
Sea beach in autumn that
Wraps me up embraced in its fold to
Hold time stands still.
Wherein vanish past, present, future.
Evaporate trace-less yet,
Strike into pores an intense intimate chord to
Make me feel to be floating aloft soft breeze,
I no longer in me absorbed and seized.

Sense of awe tossed rise and fall
In its soothing aromatic fold that
Sweetly tickles, bite and chews to be
Cleansed off inside out.
And in that what remains vague
Feels flying at ease through
Lightening and thunder
Beyond grasp of mind even to imagine.
Devoid of sense to long and belong
Wherein all vacillations
Swept out in the ether
Frees of all shackles drowned into
Infinity spread out unfathomable.
I merged in that along all known, unknown.
Aspirations and dreams.
Beginning and end.
Into unknowable unknown.

37

WE HAVE COME AND GONE

Whoever has known when time was born?
Whoever knows when life breathed its first?
Whoever can answer how and why of it all and
Why that begins must always end?
Why does it repeat over and over again?
Does Sun rise and set totally in vain?
Why flowers bloom to live so short?
Do for fun earthquake and tsunami erupt?
Do things happen unprovoked all on its own?
Questions that intrigue have answer none.
I look to the heaven for answer of it all,
Could only see that rise within finally fall.

38

THE INCOMPREHENSIBLE

Where do I begin of that
Neither has a beginning nor end that
Revolves yet stand still.
Centered yet beyond any center
Though is the essence of it all,
It itself far beyond it.
It led me through senses displaced
Even before the journey began
I lost path to get back home.

Where can I begin? If at all I can for
I am not home yet.
Any venture would be a lie to lead that
Would only push onto another to
Revolving endless around itself.
Having neither beginning nor lead
How on earth I find path lost to
Tear apart darkness that bind?

A glimpse of that in the ray of hope
I sense but can't comprehend that
Appear yet next vanish before could hold.

I realize as it dawns in me
The futility of seeking.
No seeking can ever discover any answer to that...
Neither in seeking its ever found.
Neither any effort ever can fathom nor
Speech can ever hold it in words.
Incomprehensible can only be in being
When efforts unconditionally cease
Hands rise in surrender.
Wherein silence blossoms.
Wherein one in being comprehends
The incomprehensible.

39

LONGING

Though been desperate
Longing intense to
Falling in love, been waiting for
Rains to nourish me green and
River to be in spate to flooding my heart to
Wash me through and through to be
Clean as clean can be minus any traces to
Blasting out of my unresponsive inertness.
Polish out all rusted to shine forth to sing
Matching the tune of celestial rhythm;
Embracing life loud to let heart flow out oozing,
flowing cool sparkling in moon's romantic glow to
Reaching out all set to falling in love.

The stars shining above sparkle
Glorifying celestial order.
Embraced in full Moon's glow
Soothingly spread over earth's bosom,
I am far too shaky to hold safe life's dream
So delicately woven as flower petal.
Just as nature weaves it in the bud and
My apprehension seeking a heavy
chest to keeping it safe to
Absorb impact of all onslaughts that time inflicts.

Though been versed to riding well,
Scared to riding sun's horses being
Far too hot and fast that
Scares out my guts to keep pace lest they
Ride over my dreams, shearing out
Its tender petals way before it may bloom.

Let love blossom tuned up to being my heart.
Apprehension grow what if
Stars above grow inimical and
Hit hard at that hurts most to
Shattering my dreams so far held in heart,
Throwing me back to that I may belong.

My shoulders have drooped carrying
the weight of my loneliness that
Drag my aching bones to breaking point, still
I run breathless over to hill top for a fill of fresh air,
to cool off mounted heat with all inflicted odds.
I stretch out cool fanned by
soft breeze blowing sweet that
Blow me out to fall asleep happily floating
In its sweet motion totally seized.
Just then dreaming it dawned
That no condition can
Ever let love to spark.
I must flow unrestrained
gushing down in torrents
Just as a mountain stream.
Drowning all distinctions to
Break cage to set free heart.
Let unbound it be freed of all bondage to
let love burst forth into a Niagara
In its pristine glory.
Let Moon rise divine
Even it be a no moon day to
Holding me out in trance
In its enchanting soothing embrace to
Let love flow out in me through every pore.

———∘∘∘〖◎〗∘∘∘———

40

GROWING UP BEEN...

Growing up been so far just to
Matching the ways of the world.
I am tired of equations to
Chasing this and chasing that,
Thoroughly exhaust me in and out.
Lying in the open,
Under the vast spread of mighty sky I find
The blue evening suddenly lit up in me
under the bewitching glitter of countless stars.
It delightfully led me to gaze at the abstraction that
The Nature in the collective spread that
culminated into reflecting the whole.
It transported me to a zone far,
far away from the known,
Landing me almost into trance
lost in its heavenly glory.
Fully absorbed I was freed of mind's scrutiny.

So much so that it seemed of no
concern to being alive or dead.
Hardly I had any clue of time and
space until stars above
Gently pulled me still further up into their midst
to roam free joyfully drifting unbound by will.
Happiness sizzling within never known before.
Riding horses formed in flaming
clouds that galloped soundless
Through starlit sky and I felt to being
a celestial being far away from
home and the World and everything
that poisoned, tore apart my heart.
Well, for a change all apprehension melted free.
Force risen thunder like inflamed shattered all
Bolts blown out of blue that floated me feather like
pleasantly breathed in me never known ecstasy.
Not being still sure, what is it that
made me to deserve to
Rising over gain and loss to being my own little self to
Afford breathing free just as I ever wished to
Play with the stars glowing along in them,
Gleefully befriended to playing in the wild with
Elephants and tigers, deer and leopards as
I would play with my dog.

Flying with birds and flying at will high up in sky,
Shouting loud care free, jumping up over tall trees to
Fondly looking down childlike at the mother earth.
Dread ridden joy flooding free in hearts
In pronounced togetherness to never being alone.
Heart singing loud floating on winds,
barriers broken breathing free in all and
All in me far away from dread of
network built routine.

The thought rise sudden that traumatically siege ;
Has it all been real or dream?
It strikes shiver, the very thought alone...
I fervently prayed not to be thrown
back to the dreaded.
Knowing not how must I pray, I prayed
In His name wherever He be to
Bless me to be out of the dread to let
Grow and glow to being myself
Without being pushed to be x y z,
Dragged into the lure that great men reflect
Even if it costs me to lose I am.
Oh, I am tired of being taught constant
To doing this and that to becoming great to
Tread path great soul did to growing great.

How can life be induced to being merely
A guided tour to tread on the preset
Arbitrarily drawn that agitates heart
Pushes mind to revolt.
No, for heaven sake I wish not to be programmed,
Spelt out to imitate to being this and that
To trading the soul to glamorize cage
In being that knowing I am not.
Acting out never been my cup of tea.
Hence mighty teachers of the world I pray,
Let me alone to wander my world midst star to
Find my haven as God may have planned.

———◦◦◦〗◎〖◦◦◦———

41

IT ENDS LIKE IT BEGINS

It ends like it begins yet
Each end hits a new beginning
Just as dawn in the sunset
May dream repeatedly dreamt
Over yesterday of tomorrow.
But then the surfaced may not
Match the dreamt;
Neither the sunshine that
In being caught into a vortex
Now churned, now beaten...
May hold out history neat to repeat
Breathing past into present to
Hold future in its grip.
Wherein time more often than not
Run through harsh winter only to be
Be baked next under scorching sun.

It makes even birds and animal flee to
Seeking safer haven.
Slip away safe of that strike cruel.
That burst forth sudden reaping
Rhyme and reason apart.
Clueless of how and why and who
Sets it all into motion to let loose devil,
Just when its blowing soft and cool
Grown green divine, dreaming sweet....

Lived through it all I understand well
That dawn merges not always onto sunshine.
I need die hard to all yesterdays gathered to
Living over the dead breathing clean unbeaten to
Relocating dawn anew dreamt in the sunset.

42

KNOW NOT WHAT, HOW AND WHY

Know not what, how and why
Life grown generous sudden.
Sparks out to exalt every pore that
Even the mystery perpetuating
Throws open all its windows and doors.
That never ever could be had with
all pleas put forth begging.
In it remains all that been never exposed,
Untraceable, clueless intact.

The vast mighty sky in its endless
Unfathomable stretch,
Blurs vision lost turning me into
A mere invisible dot merged in it that
Stretches onto an inconceivable vast spread.

Audacity driven mad, I venture to grip it all that
Feels like river burst forth flooded sudden.
It blasts me out clean expanded into ocean to
Being that drown all that divide
Integrated into being indivisibly one.

43

FREEDOM OUGHT BE A MYTH

Years have rolled away non-stop
In the constant flow of time and we all
Like dumb spectator witness it all.
Sometime concerned, at times restless and
Most of the time indifferent in being helpless.
Flowing away with the current hardly knowing
Where to where we are being taken away?
When I pause to look within to figure
Who is flowing away to where and why and to what?
Find answer none that may break away riddle to
setting free to live freedom unhindered
shining forth brightened in its glory.

Alas, there are none to living world
Except that lead to confound at large.
I guess in seeing it all cooked in dreams to live;
Freedom ought be a myth man craves for
Though through life its never ever achieved.

44

ASK ME NOT

Ask me not why I write?
Answer I have none and neither
I ever seek any.
Seeded womb swells up.
Ask me not why?
How and where from
It routes to expressing life
That grows within itself?
Moment to moment till time ripens to
Surface in that it holds no choice.
Energy concentrate must explode when it must.

I have witnessed it all
Awestruck ages through.
Continuity bouncing back double
Making beginning again and again,
over and over balancing imbalance perpetuate
between You in me, we in all that
Must get washed clean drowned into timeless.
Where from it flows.
Wherein it stops.
Wherein all noise end.
In being that it expands.
In that to being I am to
weed out that I am not.

45

GODS OF THE LAND

I have known the gods of the land,
Watching them from far and near and
Have known them to knowing
What befalls in knowing them.

A breed apart they rise
Bred centered into itself who
Perpetuate aligning realigning to
Harnessing forces that suit them best.
Though nothing new, lived through ages,
Storms get triggered by their mere gesture.
Contraptions hid camouflaged under their skin
Devastates life and land at a flick of their finger.
Stink emanating from ugliness flow unrestrained
Hit earth and sky hitting life at large spread all over.

46

CHILDHOOD

Never knew when did it begin that vanished
As fast before one could realize to being it was gone.
Never to return, lost into abyss of
time's unfathomable depth.
Leaving behind traces of vague memory
that fondly strikes to seeing
All its varying pranks and mischief
that in being caught
Blurted out pleas always the same
to reflecting its innocence,
As if whatever happened been just
as everything happens.

Slipping out quiet to running about
under scorching sun,
Sweating out under a shady tree
to weaving dreams that
Had never no correlate neither to present nor future
Nor to the present but only to dreaming that had
Neither head nor tail but a structure drawn out vague
In endless pattern all woven into abstraction yet
So alive it breathed into heart almost touching it to
Set the wilderness mighty alive in
being fully awakened to core.

Ever since its glory lost into
oblivion, heart has failed to
Trace back those dreams blown away
in the mighty flow of time that
Lived once awakened to life came
about naturally at ease.
It's Incomprehensible now since
head grown worldly wise that
All years added to achieve can't device
a way to relive its glamor.
Neither can it figure a way to bring back
joy lost to run childlike berserk,
Dancing wild in rain, soaked in its rhythm
Literally to being lightning and thunder
Drenched dripping wet exalted head to toe.

Defying dictate of weather fully
alive sparkling to core,
Joy oozing out of heart, to screaming free wild aloud,
Exploded into freedom, running wild
Chasing butterflies in the garden,
Playing with flowers, shoes thrown apart,
Ecstasy drenched running rain barefoot madness clad,
Splashing mud flowing along water,
Transformed into a wild world fully blossomed
Ecstasy bloomed in its pristine glory.
Living it full, fully alive unconcerned of the World
Wherein grownups live sensitivity
deprived, roughed out,
Lost to joy forever that life offers only in being a child.

Mud slung head to toe, entering
home meek and quiet
Carefully avoiding all eyes lest punishment
in wait befalls for flouting
The laid out order of the house that
Occurred fairly often that cunning
Innocence rooted could hardly ever escaped,
Yet, it had its own joy in being cuddled and kissed;
The reward came after in being punished.

Its all a dream now that was lived through once that
As of now appear so utterly vague and distant.
Memory that makes feel sad sticking faintly alive.
A picture that hazily appears as
easy vanish into oblivion.
I stand aside wondering if at all
that lived through was ever
Real or a dream that comes alive as when
A pebble is thrown onto a silent lake.

Its all over and lost, shall never ever return
Save for a glimpse that tickles now and then,
To afford a smile to often tensed self that
Rekindles the spirit to wake up the child within.

47

IN BEING GROWN STRANGER

It's been a frightfully long time
Since I met myself.
I do long and miss as much.
I understand it's shameful for
Never having time for it.
Yet, I have had time to
Meet all and sundry to
Get spent out thoroughly.
Often I ran short of time
Attending to imposed demands
Driven by ill placed courtesy even
Though load carried constant
Ached my bones;
My back and neck dented
Due my spirit over running
Which ran almost against it.
Yet, ignoring it all
Journeyed constant uphill to
Reach the summit.

A JOURNEY WITHIN

I did or didn't, matters little
At this fag end when I am
All tired and lost.
It's a tall order to
Seek out myself that I
See clear even though may look
Taller than in being at the summit.
Where can I seek it out now?
Where can it be midst
crowd collected life long?

I so desperately long to
Sit quiet to being me with it to
Breaking down the long drawn silence
Broken down to be one with it.
But no, in being frightfully drawn apart
Through and through in being ill placed that
I ended up chasing glory to ill place it?
It dawns clean on me now ;
Its none but me though
Its too late to brooding over the lost.
It is what it is that turned me
A stranger to myself.
Know not if there be any option to
Retrace it back and neither
Know how beginning afresh to
Hitting the earth can ever be the same
As when it emerged whole
Hitting the first ray of light on earth?

48

DREAM OF A FATHER

Be in that you may be
In thought and your dream that
Set you on to a trend
With all its rise and fall, let
In being indifferent to it all,
Your vision get set onto
Translate that have
Appeared impossible that
Done at ease would
Surprises you in
Knowing your strength.
Discovering of that you knew not to
Get to know that deterred you to scale
Those steep hills that
Every time you ventured,
Stood mighty to block your way to
Sinking your spirit.
Your strength led to being
Perennially undermined.

You remain stranger to your strength
In knowing your ability and skill that
Stayed dormant due ignorance of that
When it rises, it can raise the hills to the ground,
Soak up the sea dry, Tear up the
sky to reveal its mystery.
When hands act unshaken can blast it all.
In the done is revealed your strength.
You would know in witnessing it all that
Would always draw you closer to
Knowing yourself.

You are capable of surfacing it all that have
Stayed hidden dormant in you.
All you need is to dive deep within to
Know what it holds for you.
As well that hold you up.
Geared up terrain that appeared
Nonnegotiable would open up obliged
its gate unasked.
You would realize, how easily it all
Surrender to your spirit that
Stands out formidably tall
In being impenetrable and beyond.
It gave way when you simply barged into it
Saluting your unshakable faith that
Ever persisted in you unbent to
Break all that appeared unbreakable.

Let not height strike any
Phobia to scare.
There are none that be
Unconquerable.
In getting to know tools
You are blessed with;
You would know that nothing
Can measure your strength that
Handles all at ease with mere
Few drops of sweat that may
Drip over your brow only to
Let you know of your worth when
Built in myths around get
Shattered blasted out.

Think big, bigger than Universe.
For you being bigger than all
That Universe may hold.
Created can never be
Greater than the creator.
Hence grow within you to
Hold it all in your grip.

Let it be pronounced in love
That being even vaster
Than all visible and invisible that
Expanded embraces cool all in its fold.
May you be freed of all duality that
Limits and shrinks you giving way to conflict.
Guard over that cloud vision.

That mislead you to know that you are.
You are way beyond and over of it all.
Reap happy you earned.
In earning you reap
That's rightfully yours.
Your birth right to be Yourself to
Hold Universe in your grip.

Do it but not to prove to the world,
But to get to yourself to knowing you are.
That looked impossible was
A mere thought;
Harped over constant was
Compounded to look impossible.
Let your life force rise like a tornado to
Shattering it all.
Let your spirit burst out
Oozing out its aroma to
Spread out all over,
Fully blown and blossomed to
Embracing life vigor spelt out to the brim to
Gush forth free unrestrained.

49

NOTHING MORE,
NOTHING LESS

Believe me, this World is the World that
Eyes see seemingly is that it sees to
Conclude nothing less, nothing more.
All talks that rise to define and speculate that
Perpetuate for and against
In search of wisdom been that so far been
Needle lost in the haystack in the dead of night that
Springs stories, bull-shit flung all over that
Reverberate hitting all corners; Over
The hills, the sea, that live in dead as well in living...
Though blinding smoke die out
finally rising high up into sky
Yet, leave behind stink to keep pervading over earth.

Sea is sea and remains so even if
you merrily fish like swim.
Yet, you are neither the sea nor fish but
Lord pronounced to lord over all that

Owns the world, the sea the earth and the sky.
Including elements that thrive in you,
Yet, when lost, you are done for, burst out
Flattened, vision shifted outright contrary to held.
The heaven entertains no room for error and
Neither the one carrying your soul can ever
Hold you intact in that it's housed.
Heaven has no room to tolerance limit either.
Every note misspelt disrupts rhythm of
Symphony heaven composes....

Do what you will, drunk into your lordship
Shiva's Tandav ignited shall
Explode and shatter it all.
Elements connecting life spread over Universe
In entirety onto uncountable many.
In being what it is, life offers nothing free.
The world in you is the World you are that
Rise and fall along the tide you float in.
The tides are tides stirred within carry
Such spark that even can burn out the inflammable.
The air into fire into ocean into earth that
Sky witnesses dumb!

—◦◦◦◦⟆◉⟅◦◦◦—

50

CONVENIENCE

Some argue it's the age.
Some explain it's the effect of that
Time constantly weaves.
Many explain in many ways,
Some weird, some clever, some strange and yet
Some blare it out contented entertaining
Logic in the hearsay that
Float easy everywhere; On land, in air,
In the known, unknown from mouth to mouth to
reflecting knowledge that ignorance flare up.
That shroud over earth and sky.
Wherein mind float clung to surface
Knowing fully well it never can fathom
Deep into that; That may or may not be.
Whatever it be so long it knits well.
Who cares it be or not to rid of intrigue that
Persists perpetuating unprovoked.

In that life grows casually random.
But call it not casual, even if it
Swings rootless drifting along the wind
So long it hurts not the convenient
Simplifying that be unlivable.
Let surfaced be what it may.
Who cares so long it hurts not the rhythm
Life has fallen in tune to reaching
Somewhere even though
It be no destination;
Movement is what matters that
Overcomes all disagreeable stir
That override and corrode.
Let it not strike deep down the skin to
Prevent surfaced to heal up.
What matters is to live safe.
Who cares what exists or exists not.
Be it here and now or beyond.
Who cares to opening the locks
So long mind content to
Holding keys to doors don't exist.

51

HEART CRAVES TO SING

Grown constant stranger
Inside out,
It dawns on me
I have lived life of ease long,
Faces in tall names to be
The lure to being the force
Will reinforced to
Living tall to be looked at
Awe struck head raised
Rising along Sun until it sets...

Yet, awareness to that
Being nameless
Lurks within that
In being the shadow
Chases itself constant.
Persists against odds that
Blow out frequent
Into a weird apprehension in
Treading path to nowhere.

Propelled with that stir and
As it gathers momentum
Letting loose myself I rise
Despite all mounted scare
Sail along absorbing
All its bouncing jolts to
Silently dare to dive
Into fathomless to
Being myself.

Deflated in and out, I
Float in embrace of the sky.
Rocked along tides soft breeze blown,
I discover to being the song
Heart ever craved to sing.
And I sing and sing proud
Ecstasy drenched I rise
Fully alive in namelessness.

52

KNOW NOT IF I AM MOVING FORWARD OR RECEDING BACKWARDS

Words can't fathom to express mind as
Mind equally can't fathom itself diving deep.
It merely lingers on the surface ever
Unaware of its depth. Living shallow lets
Waves erupt free that keep bouncing back and forth
striking hard at its shore acting and reacting to
Its motion's dictate just as I move
unaware of where to being led.
Courage fails to dare to
Flowing against the current that
Gush in hard unwarned,
Deprive me right to quit.

When eyes turn backwards,
Mind is blurred out hit by waves that
bounce back double hitting harder still
Over and over ceaseless nonstop.
Where from the words emerge that venture to
Pushing back already dried out river to
Flow back to its origin?
Where be the origin that push it?

Where from it gathers energy to strike to
Compounding its operations to grow anarchical?
If answer could be had, may be
It would blur not my vision to wonder;
Why that begin always end to roll over back
Staged farcical even that be tragic that
Repeated over, arrive and depart,
merge in and merge out only to
Reemerge with still greater intensity?

I wish could agree or disagree to all that
I am made to witness constant since
I hardly can face all emerge.
I am a traveler on the run
Wandering still unaware of my destination.
I see the seed that fall from the tree that
Knows not it contains the very tree it fell from.
Neither the tree realize it's risen from
Very seed it has grown.

Mystery wrapped in the invisible persists that
Confound all effort to govern that governs it all.
It's tricky, it's slippery shrouded over and over
In uncountable layers that makes the horse to
Keep pulling the cart until it hits its doomsday.

In being on move I see it all.
The tree in the seed and seed in the tree.
Wherein all appear bound by strange phenomena.
Wherein river is sucked in to become the sea.

Stuck between the beginning and end that
In being and being not split me multiplied into many,
Throw me to wonder if in that I seem to exist
Moving forward or
Receding backward or
Direction lost awe struck
Just standing still...